Fuck This Shit

Vulgar Activities For Procrastinators

Featuring 100 Adult Activities Such As:
Word Searches, Dot-to-Dot, Mazes, Fallen
Phrases, Math Logic, Spot the Difference,
Word Tiles, Word Scramble, Cryptogram,
Sudoku, Draw the Squares, Zig Zag and
Games to Play with a friend.

Thank you for your goddamn purchase!!
I hope you enjoy this fucking fun as hell book,
each page has its own damn impressive activity.

If you leave a review on Amazon and email me to let
me know, I will send you a free paperback copy of any
book of your choice from my Amazon collection!

http://www.amazon.com/T.L.-Adams/e/B00YSROGC4

tamaraadamsauthor@gmail.com

www.tamaraladamsauthor.com

https://twitter.com/@TamaraLAdams

https://www.facebook.com/TamaraLAdamsAuthor/

https://www.pinterest.com/Tjandlexismom/tamara-l-adams-author/

Acknowledgments: Some images for the activities were downloaded from
Publicdomainvectors.org and I appreciate all they have on their website!

It's a Fallen Phrase, Bitch

Answer on page 101

A fallen phrase puzzle is a shit puzzle where all the letters have fallen to the bottom. They got mixed up on their way down, but remain in the same damn row. Complete the fucked puzzle by filling the letters into the column they fall under. You start by filling in the one-letter columns (easy as fuck), because those don't have anywhere else to go in their column. Also try filling in common one-, two- and three-letter words as shown in the example below.

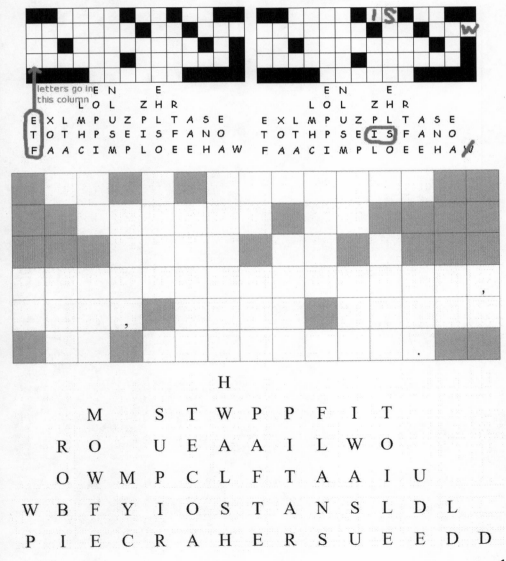

1

Draw the other half of this sad sack, then add your own touches to help procrastinate the shit out of the day!

Find the 11 phones in the image

Answer on page 101

Then go make a damn phone call
So you can waste away the time.

Solve this damn Maze already!
Start at the top and work your way to the bottom

Answer on page 101

Math Squares

Somebody fucked up this puzzle.
Try to fill in the missing numbers if you damn well can.

Use the numbers 1 through 9 to complete the equations.

Each row is a goddamn math equation. Work your way from left to right. And don't fucking cheat.

But that's not all, bitch! Each column is it's own shit math equation. Work that shit from top to bottom.

9	/		+	8	11
-		x		/	
	-	4	x		6
+		/		+	
5	-		x	1	-1

7		2		5

Answer on page 101

Color this shit to help waste away some damn time:

Fix this shit: The goal is to figure out how to fit the numbered bricks into the square of shit bricks without changing their shape or breaking them into pieces.

| 7 | 7 | 7 | | 3 | 3 | 3 |

| 7 | 5 | 5 | | | 6 | 6 | 6 |

| 11 | | 5 | | 2 | | 6 | 6 |

| 11 | | 5 | | 2 | 2 | | 6 |

| | | 5 | | | | | |

| 1 | 1 | | | 4 | 4 | 4 |

| 1 | 1 | 1 | | | 4 | 8 |

| 10 | 10 | | 9 | | 9 | 8 |

| 10 | 10 | | 9 | | 9 | 8 |

| 10 | 10 | | 9 | 9 | 9 | 8 |

Cryptogram

Answer on page 101

You are given this crap piece of text where each letter is substituted with a number and you need to goddamn decide which letters in the alphabet are being coded by the numbers you are given. You need to use logic to crack this fucked code. Example is given below:

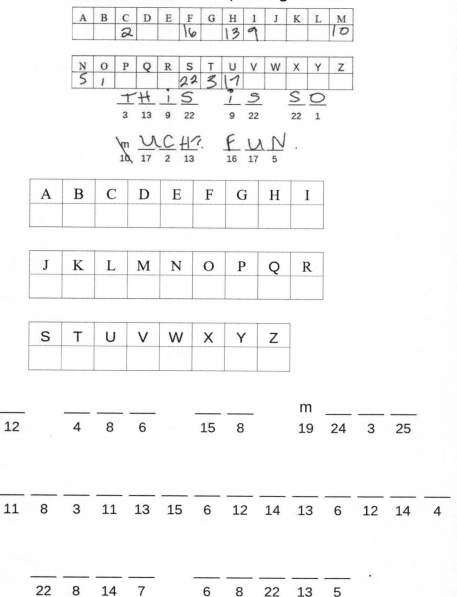

A	B	C	D	E	F	G	H	I	J	K	L	M
		2			6		13	9				10

N	O	P	Q	R	S	T	U	V	W	X	Y	Z
5	1				22	3	7					

T H I S   I S   S O
3 13 9 22   9 22   22 1

M U C H?   F U N.
10 17 2 13 16 17 5

A	B	C	D	E	F	G	H	I

J	K	L	M	N	O	P	Q	R

S	T	U	V	W	X	Y	Z

___ ___ ___ ___   ___ ___   m ___ ___ ___
12   4   8   6   15   8   19 24 3 25

___ ___ ___ ___ ___ ___ ___ ___ ___ ___ ___ ___ ___ ___ ___
20 11 8   3 11 13 15 6 12 14 13 6 12 14 4

___ ___ ___ ___   ___ ___ ___ ___ ___
22 8 14 7   6   8 22 13 5

Find the one prick below that matches the asshole bastard shadow here on the left

Answer on page 101

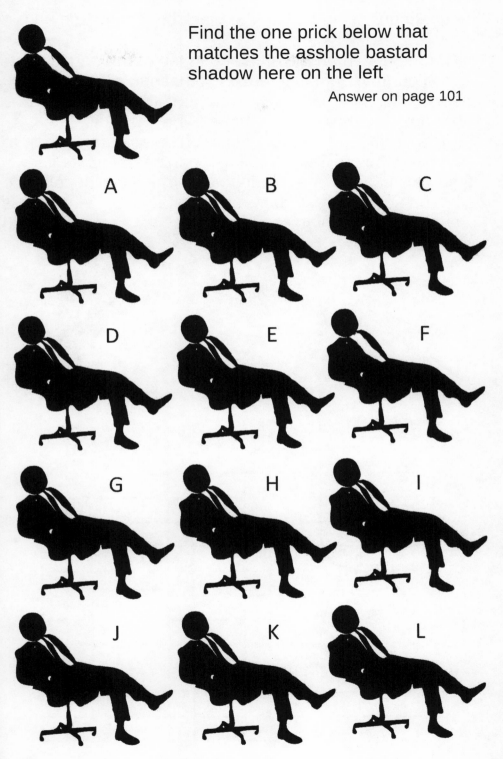

A

B

C

D

E

F

G

H

I

J

K

L

The goal consists in finding the black boxes in each grid.

The figures given on the side and in top of the grid indicate the numbers of black boxes in that line or column.

For damn example 3,3 on the left of a line indicates that there is, from left to right, a block of 3 black boxes then a second block of 3 black boxes on the same shite line.
To solve a puzzle, one needs to determine which cells will be boxes and which will be empty. Determining which cells are to be left empty is as important as those to be filled.

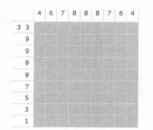 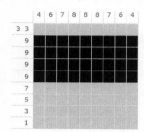 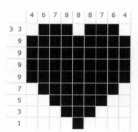

Answer on page 101

	5	1, 1	1, 1	1, 2, 1, 1	1, 2, 2, 1, 1	1, 1, 1, 1	1, 2, 2, 1, 1	1, 2, 2, 1, 1	1, 1, 1	1, 1	5
5											
1, 1											
1, 1											
1, 2, 2, 1											
1, 3, 3, 1											
1, 1											
1, 1											
1, 5, 1											
1, 1											
1, 1											
5											

Zig Zag game

Complete the 6-letter word at the top of each diagram. Use the last two letters of the first word as the first two letters of the second word If you get fuckin stuck, try starting at the damn bottom of the diagram and working your way up, in reverse.

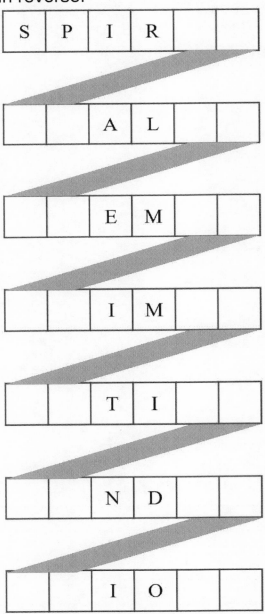

Answer on page 102

Number Blocks

Try to fill in all the bastard missing numbers.

The missing numbers are integers from 1 to 9.
The numbers in each row add up to totals to the right.
The numbers in each column add up to the totals along
the bottom. I know it's a lot but it's better than work!
The diagonal lines also add up the totals to the right.
Now get your shit together and procrastinate!

					22
3		5	8		20
2	1				16
	7		2		22
1		8			20
10	18	28	22		18

Answer on page 102

Take your damn time unscrambling all of the words that will help you waste a way the hours so you don't have to do actual shit work.

1. ctinrasatoper   _____

2. neednuccorn   _____

3. tenthsuunsicia   _____

4. lemonlichac   _____

5. riftneedfin   _____

6. caldickaalias   _____

7. napesaidsisot   _____

8. distedsternie   _____

9. predicdjuneu   _____

10. soonlistcade   _____

11. gushlininga   _____

12. funportcrye   _____

12. invitetaten   _____

12. hollymenac   _____

Answer on page 102

Letter Tiles

Have some fucking fun moving all the damn tiles around to make the correct stupich phrase. The three letters on each tile must stay together and in the given order. Cheating won't help your ass with this one.

P R	V E	I N A	N I S	K I
S O M	O F	H A	S T E	O C R
Y .	I L L	T I N	I	T R O M
H I N	G T	A S T	R D A	E U
Y E	N F I	S T	O D	H E D

Answer on page 102

Search for the fucking inspiring words

lackluster   lifeless   limp

postpone   slothful   low

subdued   mopy   tame

unmoved   dawdle   cool

hesitate   dally

```
      N G G J O P                           D H E S O P
  E   T R C X E O P                     U   T E E X B N M
  N   V A S O P L D Z               M   P U D N B V X Q
  O   T A M E N M L J H         I   J P C O I Y T E S
  O   K E B V X Q O R V H J B V E N O P T S O P F H X
  Q   O F Y T E Y X V P M J H P C O L N B P Q V P U K
  B   W U P F O X S R Y I K H F R V C O P L P L M N C
  I   D L V U I K L O F T W T I O P R W X D A L G M M
  A   P P S M M C E T U O L C G P F H J K E Y R D O V
  P   U R S D C M L O G F C W X D A L L Y R X E I V M
  P   I Y R E X V N J L M E W S Z U V W S P E S O E L
  B   C X E U P M Z W U A X I O S W P L M N E X B D M
  N   V E S D P T D Z Q G C N M L J H F D M N B V X Q
  O   T E X B N N L J H F D K Q W R V H J H I Y T E S
  R   K N B U X A W R V H J B L X V P M J G O P F H P
  G   E I Y S E L X V P M L U F U T N U O B Q V P L C
      D T P F H I S R Y I K H K L S F T W E P L K J
        Y P I B L O W T W T C E T T O L E D U
          D Z Q G J N V X Y M H J K E S V C
      N M L J H F D S R Y I J L N B U R P C P L
    V X Q W R V H J B V C F H C O P G P F S V C H
  Y T E S X V P M J S P E P L R W X X G J P P R S O
  P F H X S R Y I S H F S M C H J K L O F I F H X B
  V P I E L O F E W T U O P O S O E L D W A D M B V
  L I N T I G L R A T E P F H S B N M L J I F T Y T
  S E C A L E G F D W X G J M B D X Q W R T U O P F
  Y I K T F S V C O P L O F T Y T N S X V E G P V P
  F T W I U O P R W X P L U F H T O L S R D L M R Y
  U O L S G P F H J K E E G F V P M J H X W U I O F
  G F D E X G J M B F S J L M R Y I K H K O U L P U
  L M E H S Z U V W S P W U V O F T W T C F M N B D
  U V X I O S W P E M Y O S M P U B E L Y C O I U T
  G J O P U R E R N L T P M N B D H S O O B C X E O
  C X E O P L P G F D     C O I       T E J B N O S P L
  S O P L D M Q G J       X Y M       D B V X E C B N M
  X B N M I J H F         Y I J       Y T E N B V X Q
  B V X Q W R V           C F H       F H I Y T E S
    T E S X V             T P Y         I O P F H
```

Answer on page 102

Draw these shit images to each of the damn squares

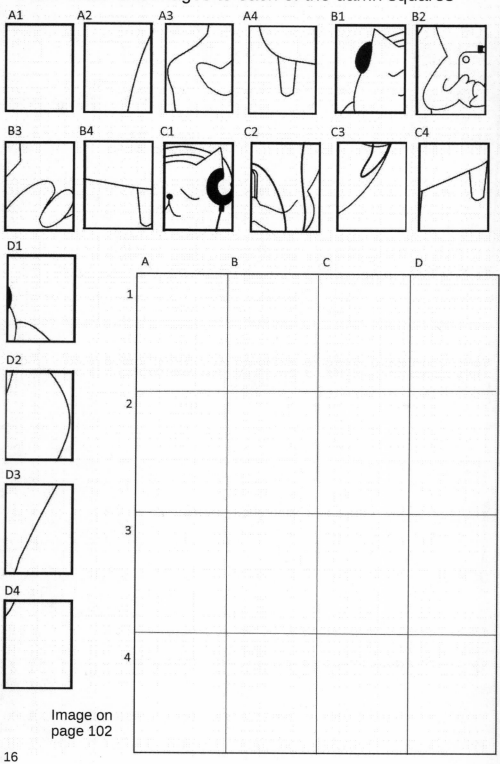

Find the 1 lonely fucker that is different from the rest

Answer on page 102

How many fucking squares can you find in the circle? It looks hard but is pretty damn easy, but at least it will help you piss away some time doing nothing important like all the shit work you should be doing!

Answer on page 102

Quest this shit!

Answer on page 103

Your fucked task is to fill every empty cell with a positive or negative integer in such a way so that each white cell's value equals the sum of its adjoining half-height cells. When complete, each Balance Quest puzzle grid will "balance" itself in such a way so that the four center cells surrounding the center "zero cell" will always add up to zero.

There are five rules that must be followed in every Quest puzzle:
The gray cells must include all integers between -16 and 16, except 0
No number can be repeated within any of the gray cells. Got That?
The number in each white cell must equal the sum of its adjoining cells. The center Zero cell is always the sum of all four adjacent cells.

** Numbers can (and will) be reused across both white and gray cells. The rules specify only that the -16 to 16 numbers can never be used more than once in the gray cells. A damn good example is below:

-8		-8+6=-2		-2+4=-2	
6	-2	-1+5=4	-2		2
5			2		
-1	4		4		

		2+-9+
2	-1	-1+8=0
	0	
-9	8	

The main puzzle grid:

- -8 | 8 | -5 | | | | | 21 | 6
- 1 | | | | | | | | 7
- -7 | | | | 42 | | | | 14
- | | | | | 9 | 1 | | -12
- -9 | -11 | | | 0 | | | |
- 8 | 5 | -23 | | | | -12 | -16
- -13 | | | -18 | | | | | 2
- 9 | | | | | | | | 3
- -4 | 6 | | | | 21 | 6 | 11

19

This bitch is just as bored as you. Find the 11 differences between the two images

Answer on page 103

Connect the dots from 100 to 135
Don't let the bastard extra numbers fool you!

218   258   243   230
101   102   268   278   240   276
257   233   103   233   248   249   245   244
105   104   264   253   242
238   106   246   245   247   264   237   241   238
246   254   250   237
243   255   255   136   272   239
251   100 108   107   279   138   186
140   274   139   236
144   254   151   145   254   185   275   166
270
271   226   111   248   249
262   265   230   258   236   168   167
110   250   112
256   238   269   241   143   212   259   257   169   272   265
243   202
259   242   109   239   113   171   247   269   266
210
239   253   115   114   262   195   239   184   241   267
244
239   214   261   222   137   147   170   268   260
223   148   237
237   236   117   118   172   250   245
259   226   256   263
236   268   225   119   271   174
235   211   196   120   121   188   263
217   212   275   236
239   277   198   122   238   175   176   240
235   141   266   116
207   173   278   261   248   178   177
210   279   215   213
142   209   146   214   271   189   199   187   179
238   124   123   182   180
234   228   265   197   276   200   267   183
260   125   126   213
263   278   217   264   206   127   275   194
266   209
149   256   231   218   129   237   249
277   220   216   128   193
270   261   227   247   270   208   274   246   252
279   229   224   274   252
262   229   238   237   228   130   191
260   225   190   131
234   224   252   244   242   135   192   251
272   220   211   227   205
257   216   258   255   231   273   132
267   276   253   273   273   215
251   204   152   134   133

Answer on page 103

21

How many words can you find within the phrase:

Leave this shit for tomorrow

1._____
2._____
3._____
4._____
5._____
6._____
7._____
8._____
9._____
10._____
11._____
12._____
13._____
14._____
15._____
16._____
17._____
18._____
19._____
20._____
21._____
22._____
23._____
24._____
25._____

These are the rules of shit sudoku

Numbers from 1 to 9 are inserted into sets that have 9 x 9 = 81 squares in whole. Every number can be used just goddamn once in every, 3x3 block, column and row.

- Every number can be used just once in the blocks of 3 x 3 = 9 square blocks. Got that shit?
- Each row of 9 numbers ought to contain all digits 1 through 9 in any order. So don't leave a damn one out.
- Every column of 9 numbers should comprise all digits 1 through 9 in any order also.

One way to figure out which numbers can go in each space is to use "process of elimination" by checking to see which other numbers are already included within each square – since there can be no duplication of numbers 1-9 within each square (or row or column).

	3	6	9					
2				8				5
			1		6	8		
	2	7	4		1		9	
	1						4	
	4		2		8	7	3	
		2	8		5			
1				3				6
					9	2	8	

Answer on page 103

Rules For Playing Numbers in a Damn Square

For this fucking bitch of a problem use only the numbers 1, 2 and 3 to solve all the shit issues in the box.
The numbers in each heavily outlined set of squares, called cages, must combine (in any order) to produce the target number in the top corner using the mathematical operation indicated (+, -, ×, ÷). Use each number only once per row, once per column. Cages with just one square should be filled in with the target number in the top corner. A number can be repeated within a cage as long as it is not in the same row or column. Did you get all that crap? Good luck!

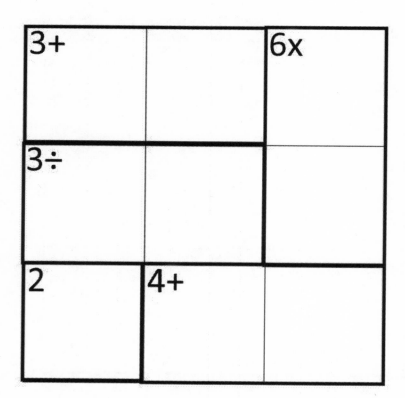

Answer on page 103

Tic Tac Toe with a friend Bitches!
Take turns placing your mark (o or x) in a square in the grid. The first person to get three in a row wins. If all 9 squares are filled in before someone gets three in a row, the game ends in a fucking tie.

Connect Four should be played with another asshole
Players take turns initialing a circle, starting with the bottom row, but players can then place discs anywhere as long as the spaces under them are filled. The shithead winner is the player who gets four discs in a vertical, horizontal or diagonal row. Keep on Procrastinating!

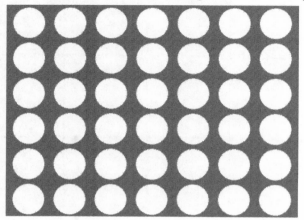

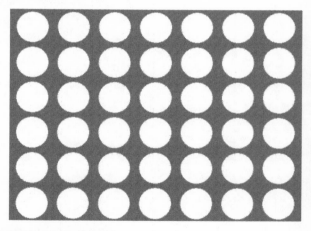

Pipelayer (And no, not the kind of pipe laying you are thinking of) player is squares the other is circles. Each player takes turns drawing a horizontal or vertical line between two of their shapes. The goal is to be the first to create a single continuous line from one edge of the grid to the other (7-units). You cannot draw one line across another, so blocking the others move can be an advantage.

Dots and Boxes, you crazy wankers, is a bitchin fun game
Take turns drawing lines between two adjacent dots with a horizontal
or vertical line. The play who completes the fourth side of the box,
initials the box and gets to draw another line. When all the boxes are
completed the winner is the player who has initialed the most boxes.

Sim (No not Sims asshole, sorry this book is not that fancy)
Players alternately join dots on a hexagon by drawing along the
lines provided; the first player who is forced to complete a triangle
in their own color is the loser in more way than one probably.

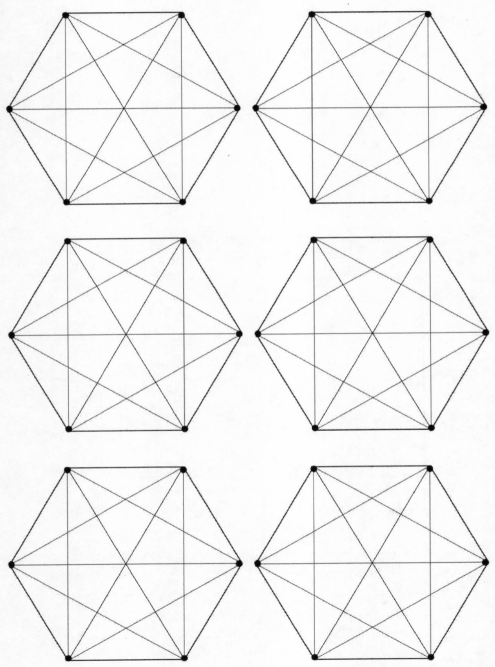

Five in a Row, is like tic tac toe but on fucking acid
The players take turns in marking a square with their x or o.
The first player to get five squares in a row, horizontally,
vertically, or diagonally, wins. (Two games here, bitches)

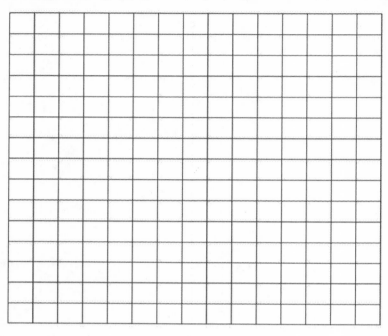

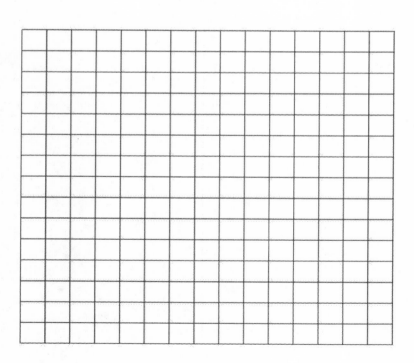

Players take turns naming a letter. As each letter is named each player must write it immediately into one of the cells in their own grid. Players can choose any letter they like, and letters can be repeated. When the grid is full the players count up the number of four-letter words they have made, reading across, down, or diagonally, and the one with the highest score wins. Tip: you can either choose letters to help you complete words, or you can try to fuck with your opponent.

This player earns 6 points with these words: CARD, TOSS, COAT, RIPS, DOTS, and CUPS

C	A	R	D
O	U	I	O
A	B	P	T
T	O	S	S

This player wins with 7 points from these words: CARP, AUTO, CATS, SOBS, PODS, POTS, STOP

C	A	R	P
A	U	O	O
T	T	I	D
S	O	B	S

Hangman (this is a fucking time suck if I ever saw one)
Each player takes a turn picking a word to spell out and draws lines underneath to represent the letters in the word. The other person guesses letters. Any letters that fit in the word, get put into the word. The other letters are placed on top above the image and parts of a stick man are drawn till either the word is guessed or stick man is complete and you are fucking out of luck.

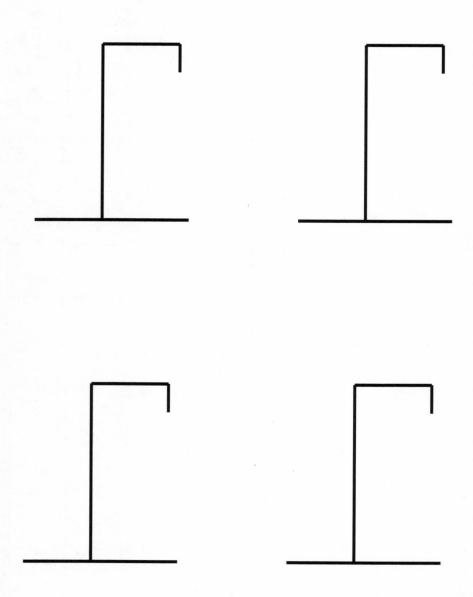

Each player takes a turn writing an 'S' or 'O' in a square. The damn goal is to complete the sequence S-O-S in three adjacent squares (vertical, horizontal, diagonal). When a player completes the SOS, they mark it as theirs. Play continues until all squares are occupied. Player with the most S-O-S sequences is the lucky as shit winner.

Procrastinate with Fallen Phrase

Answer on page 103

This is a fucked puzzle where all the wanked letters have fallen to the bottom. They got mixed up on the way down, but remain in the same bumblefuck row. You complete the puzzle by filling the letters into shit the column they fall under. You start by filling in the one-letter columns, because those assholes don't have anywhere else to go in their shit column. Also try filling in common one-, two- and three-letter words as shown in the bitchin example below.

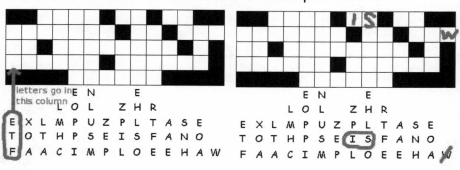

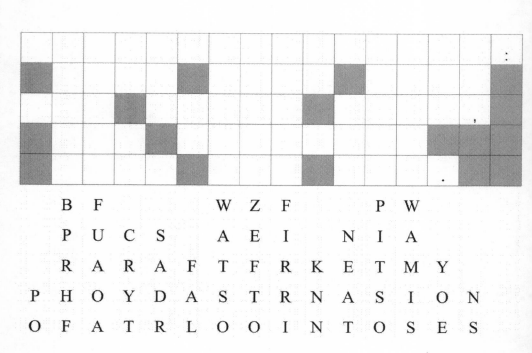

B	F				W	Z	F			P	W	
P	U	C	S		A	E	I		N	I	A	
R	A	R	A	F	T	F	R	K	E	T	M	Y
P	H	O	Y	D	A	S	T	R	N	A	S	I	O	N
O	F	A	T	R	L	O	O	I	N	T	O	S	E	S

Draw the other half of this crazy su-ka, then add your own damn touches to help procrasterbate away the time.

Wank off then find 12 pissflap pens in the image

Answer on page 103

Math Squares

Hey wicked pisser, try to fill in the missing numbers.

Use the numbers 1 through 9 to complete the equations.

Each row is a math equation. Work your way from left to right and try not to fuck up the cunt math.
Each column is a math equation. Work from top to bottom, so you got that shit to figure out too. Lucky you!

	x	9	/		**15**
x		+		+	
4	-		x	8	**-24**
/		-		/	
	-	6	+		**-3**

10 **10** **11**

Answer on page 103

Solve the wankadoodle of a maze to piss away time.
Start at the top and work your way to the bottom.

Answer on page 104

Color this shit!
Take your time, you don't have shit to do or places to go.

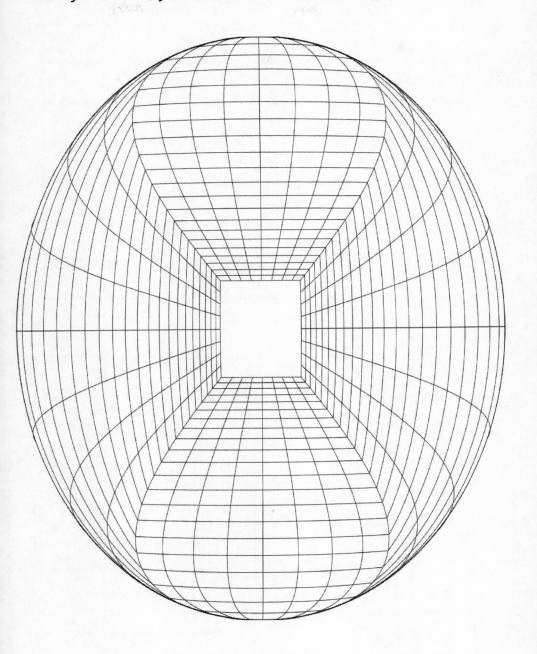

Fuck this puzzle! Figure out how to fit the numbered bricks into the square of shit bricks without changing their shape or breaking them into any fuckwit pieces.

Answer on page 104

Cryptogram

Answer on page 104

You are given this assbastard piece of text where each letter is substituted with a number and you need to decide which letters in the alphabet are being coded by the numbers you are given. An ass example is shown here:

A	B	C	D	E	F	G	H	I	J	K	L	M
		2			16		13	9				10

N	O	P	Q	R	S	T	U	V	W	X	Y	Z
5	1				22	3	17					

T H I S   I S   S O
3 13 9 22   9 22   22 1

M U C H?   F U N .
10 17 2 13   16 17 5

A	B	C	D	E	F	G	H	I

J	K	L	M	N	O	P	Q	R

S	T	U	V	W	X	Y	Z

___   ___ ___ ___   ___ ___ ___ ___ ___   ___ ___
6   17 20 18   21 7 6 25 21   16 7

p__ ___ ___ ___ ___ ___ ___ ___ ___ ___ ___ ___
15 3 7 24 3 20 18 16 6 25 20 16 19

___ ___ ___ ___ ___ ,   ___ ___ ___
16 7 12 20 9   5 23 16

___ '   ___ ___   ___ ___ ___ ___   ___ ___
6   26 26   14 23 18 16   12 7

___ ___   ___ ___ ___ ___ ___ ___ ___ ___ .
6 16   16 7 11 7 3 3 7 17

Find the one lazy motherfucker below that matches his asshole twin shadow here on the left

Answer on page 104

The shit goal is to fucking find the black boxes to color.

The figures given on the side and in top of the grid indicate the numbers of black boxes in that line or column.

For example 3,3 on the left of a line indicates that there is, from left to right, a block of 3 damn black boxes then a second block of 3 black boxes on the same crap line.
To solve a puzzle, one needs to determine which cells will be boxes and which will be empty. Determining which cells are to be left empty is as important as those to be filled.

 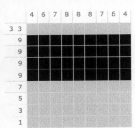 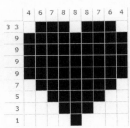

Answer on page 104

	7	1,1,1	3,3	0	7	1,1	7	0	7	1,1	3,3	0	7	1,1,1	1,1	0	7	1,1	5
3, 3, 3, 3, 2																			
1, 1, 1, 1, 1, 1, 1, 1, 1																			
1, 1, 1, 1, 1, 1, 1, 1, 1																			
2, 1, 1, 2, 2, 1 ,1																			
1, 1, 1, 1, 1, 1, 1, 1, 1																			
1, 1, 1, 1, 1, 1, 1, 1, 1																			
3, 3, 1, 1, 3, 2																			

Zig Zag is a cunt of a game

Complete the 7-letter word at the top of each diagram.
Use the last two letters of the first word as the first two
letters of the second word If you get stuck, try starting at
the bumfuck end of the diagram and working your way up
in reverse.

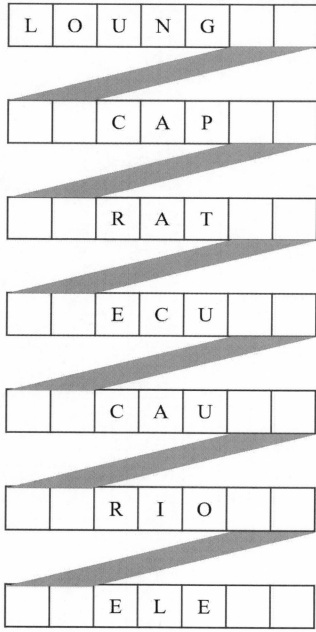

| L | O | U | N | G | | |

| | | C | A | P | | |

| | | R | A | T | | |

| | | E | C | U | | |

| | | C | A | U | | |

| | | R | I | O | | |

| | | E | L | E | | |

Answer on page 104

This Fucking Number Block again

Try to fill in some more damn missing numbers. Who the shit keeps losing these fuckers anway.

The missing numbers are integers from 1 and 9.
The numbers in each row add up to totals to the right.
The numbers in each column add up to the totals along the bottom. You know the goddamn drill by now!
The diagonal lines also add up the totals to the right.

					23
7		5		4	27
	1		2	6	23
4		6	8		28
	8	2		9	27
3	6		4		26
26	21	27	23	34	23

Answer on page 104

Letter Tiles: What the fuck happened here?

You can either masturbate your time away or move the damn tiles around to make the correct phrase. The three letters on each tile must stay together. You choose!

F E R	I N A	U C E	L M	O C R
P R	C .	I ' M	D O	D E A
D P	P R E	D L I	J U	O R K
S T	I N D	T O R	N E -	T A
I N	N O	A N I	A L	A
,	I Y	W I N G	A S T	

Answer on page 104

Find the 1 lazy bitch that is different from the others

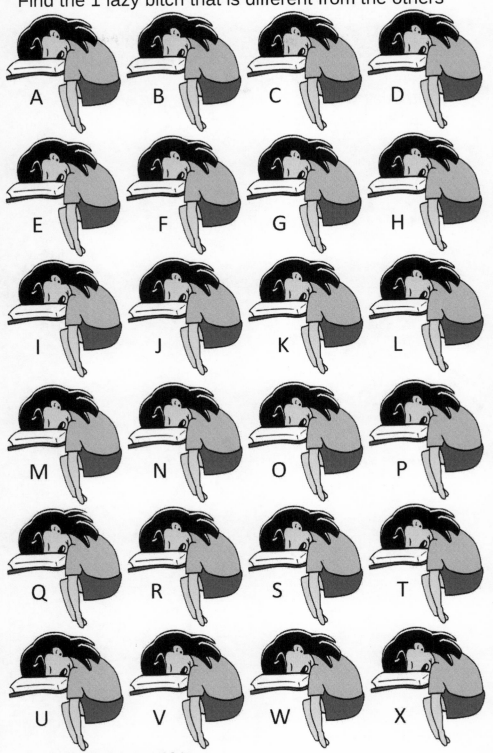

Search for the positively jizzcock words

tired   dull   aloof

casual   indifferent   neutral

negative   uncurious   withdrawn

apathetic   blah   broken

dejected   dispirited

```
            O P N D Z Q G J H F S E C N D N
          X B S M L J H F D T U R D J C E I Y
        N B E X A S L P N E K O R B O K A I P F
      O I D T R S X V P M J F D S O Y B P S W P I
  B W Z P T K           I K U H           T P U A M C
  I I Q U P             T W A O           R S A L M
  A P E L M             O L D P           Y R D L F
  P N R S E             B K O J           X E I O M
  P I Y R D             M E N Z           E S O Y L
  B C X E I             V X R S           E L B S M
  P D I S P I R I T E D J I   N J H F D M A B V T Q
  O T E X B N M D J H F       L A V M M C I Y T I S
  O K N B V X Q N R V H       X V P V N J O P F C X
  Q O R Y T E S Y V T M       S R E V I T A G E N K
  B W O I F H X R R Y I       L O F J W N L L M M C
  I D Q V P I K L O F T R C E T C F H X B N V N J
  A P P V X S W R T U O L E L I T I M B V X I H J
  M U N C U R I O U S F D V D J L F T Y T E J W N
  S R P F H X S D M N V X M H J K U O E F H H C O
  X B M M L J                         H P L R W
  B D U L L                           T C H J
  Y T E S M                           P A S O
  P D H X S                           G H P B
  V P E K L O F T W T U O R S O P P T P L O M B A
    M M J E T J P L T N E R E F F I D N I T T Y
      C M E O G F D W X G M B V X Q R R T U O
        H F C V C O P L O T Y T E S X O O G
          U O T R W I T H D R A W N S R C
            P F E J K E N Q S T O J H X
              J M D F R J M R Y I K H
```

Answer on page 105

Unscramble each of the dickwad words instead
of helping out your asshole co-worker

1. loak hec htctcw   _____

2. lad-lilydly   _____

3. rad mounbu   _____

4. daldlid-deded   _____

5. loud ofarno   _____

6. water fritay   _____

7. straw nofet ghee   _____

8. noft fured   _____

9. foof fog   _____

10. hand grunoa   _____

11. hot nagu   _____

12. fot puf   _____

12. ground scoreuna   _____

12. hang lopsle   _____

Answer on page 105

This Quest is a Motherfucking Procrastinators Dream!

Your task is to fill every empty cell with a positive or negative integer in such a way so that each white cell's value equals the sum of its adjoining half-height cells. When complete, each Balance Quest puzzle grid will "balance" itself in such a way so that the four center cells surrounding the center "zero cell" will always add up to zero.

There are five rules that must be followed in every Quest puzzle:
The gray cells must include all integers between -16 and 16, except 0
No number can be repeated within any of the gray cells.
The number in each white cell must equal the sum of its adjoining cells. The center Zero cell is always the sum of all four adjacent cells.

** Numbers can (and will) be reused across both white and gray cells. The rules specify only that the -16 to 16 numbers can never be used more than once in the gray cells. Example is below:

-8		-8+6=-2
6	-2	-1+5=4
5		
-1	4	

-2	
	2
4	

-2+4=-2

2	
	0
-9	

	-1
8	

2+-9+
-1+8=0

12	13						18	13
-5		4						-10
11					4			-11
	7					-8	12	14
10				0				
-12	-3							-8
-6		-24					9	6
-13			-52					
-7	-23					37	6	16
								7

Answer on page 105

How many damn words can you find below?

Answer on page 105

Can't draw? Who the fuck cares. You can't make it worse

A1 A2 A3 A4

B1 B2 B3 B4

C1 C2 C3 C4

D1 D2 D3 D4

	A	B	C	D
1				
2				
3				
4				

Image on page 105

Connect the dots from 100 to 118. Don't let the shite extra numbers fool you into making a damn mistake!

230
218   258   268   278   240   247   276   243
224   233   248   249   245   244
254   233   242   238
223   246   110   253   127   238
246   346   245   123   111   272   237
238   109   243   255   250
137   255   122   112
251   257   254   279   119   274   172
108   270   226   248   185   275   166   236
271   120
262   265   230   254   236   168   167   249
238   264   121   258   257   169   265
256   269   250   259   272
259   241   212   243
107   239   247   266
239   136   241   214   171   210   269
244   236   267
242   253   262   125   239   170   241
239   222   268   260
264   237   261   195   113
237   106   226   250   245
236   259   196   256   263
268   225   239   271   174
235   105   277   114   275   188   263
217   212   104   236
270   211   210   198   173   175   176   240
235   266   207   209   238
242   278   261   248   178   177
279   215   213   271   187
276   189   199   179
197   238   214   224   186
234   260   182   180
260   228   265   103   273   184   183
278   217   124   206   200   215   194   213
263   266   264   273   275
131   256   231   218   249
277   220   216   209   267   237
270   261   102   115   208   274   246   252   193
262   279   130   227   247   229   116   202   274   252
101   129   238   237   228   225   190   192   251
128   234   100   244   191
237   118   126   117   227   211
272   216   258   255   205   231
267   257   253   132   273   229
252   204

Answer on page 105

53

How many words can you find within the words:

Work is for Assholes

1._____
2._____
3._____
4._____
5._____
6._____
7._____
8._____
9._____
10._____
11._____
12._____
13._____
14._____
15._____
16._____
17._____
18._____
19._____
20._____
21._____
22._____
23._____
24._____
25._____

These are the fucking annoying rules of sudoku

Numbers from 1 to 9 are inserted into sets that have 9 x 9 = 81 squares in whole. Every number can be used just once in e-furry, 3x3 block, column and row.

- Every number can be used just an once in the blocks of 3 x 3 = 9 square blocks. Got it? Good!
- Each row of 9 numbers ought to contain all digits 1 through 9 in any order. Is this shit clear?
- Every column of 9 numbers should comprise all digits 1 through 9 in any order. Have I lost your ass yet?

One way to figure out which numbers can go in each space is to use "process of elimination" by checking to see which other numbers are already included within each square – since there can be no duplication of numbers 1-9 within each square (or row or column).

	7	3		4	6	9		
		2			9	3		
		9					7	2
9					8			4
	2						3	
3			7					1
5	9					2		
		1	3			7		
		8	9	1		4	6	

Answer on page 106

Find the 12 shit differences between the two lazy asses

Answer on page 106

Rules For Playing Numbers in a shit Square

For this problem use only the numbers 1, 2, 3 and 4 to solve. The numbers in each heavily outlined set of squares, called cages, must combine (in any order) to produce the target number in the top corner using the mathematical operation Indicated (+, -, ×, ÷). Is this shit fucked or what? Use each number only once per row, and also only fucking once per column. Cages with just one square should be filled in with the target number in the top corner. A number can be repeated within a cage as long as it is not in the same row or column. I'm lost too, but hey at least it's not work.

2-	2-		8x
	3	1-	
8x	3+		
		4+	

Answer on page 106

Tic Tac Toe like a crazy mother fucker!
Take turns placing your mark (o or x) in a square in the grid. The first person to get three in a row wins. If all 9 squares are filled in before someone gets three in a row, the game ends in a tie.

Connect Four if you can bitches
Players take turns initialing a circle, starting with the bottom row, but players can then place discs anywhere as long as the spaces under them are filled. The asshole winner is the player who gets four discs in a vertical, horizontal or diagonal row.

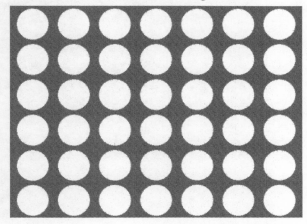

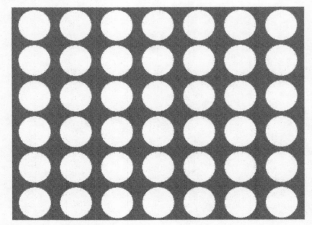

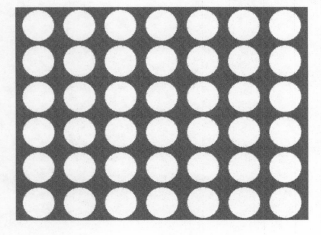

Pipelayer (Get your mind out of the gutter is a game-Two Games)
One player is squares the other is circles. Each player takes turns
drawing a horizontal or vertical line between two of their shapes.
The goal is to be the first to create a single continuous line from one
edge of the grid to the other (7-units). You cannot draw one line
across another, so blocking the others move can be an advantage.

Dots and Boxes (Or you can draw a dick in a box for fun)
Take turns drawing lines between two adjacent dots with a horizontal
or vertical line. The play who completes the fourth side of the box,
initials the box and gets to draw another line. When all the boxes are
completed the winner is the player who has initialed the most boxes.

Sim (This shit is not simple so get your fucking head together)
Players alternately join dots on a hexagon by drawing along the
lines provided; the first player who is forced to complete a triangle
in their own color is the goddamn loser of the bunch.

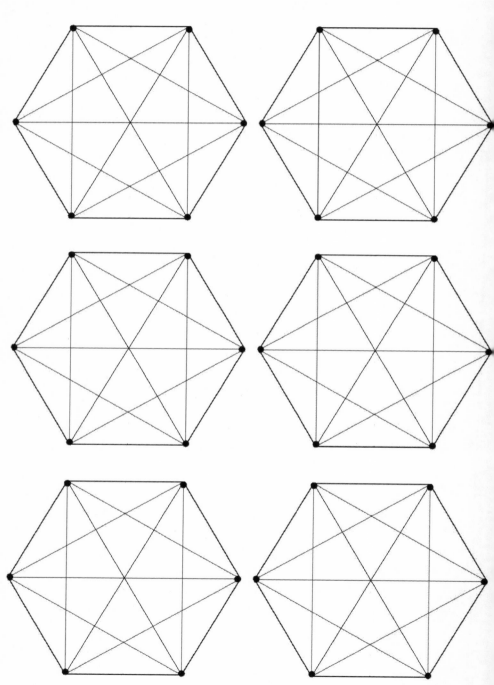

Five in a Row (Like Tic Tac Toe on fucking steroids)
The players take turns in marking a square with their x or o.
The first player to get five squares in a row, horizontally,
vertically, or diagonally, wins. (Two games here)

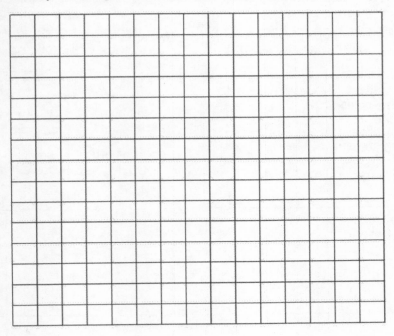

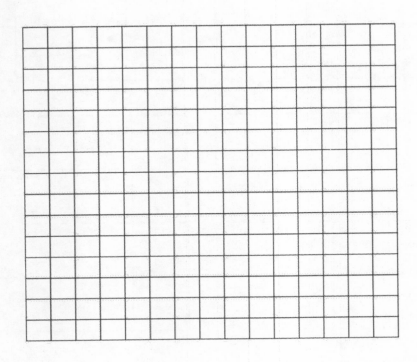

Players take turns in naming a letter. As each letter is named each player must write it immediately into one of the cells in their own grid Players can choose any letter they like, and letters can be repeated. When the grid is full the players count up the number of four-letter words they have made, reading across, down, or diagonally, and the one with the highest score wins. Tip: you can either choose letters to help you complete words, or you can try to fuck with your opponent's words.

This player earns 6 points with these words: CARD, TOSS, COAT, RIPS, DOTS, and CUPS

C	A	R	D
O	U	I	O
A	B	P	T
T	O	S	S

This player wins with 7 points from these words: CARP, AUTO, CATS, SOBS, PODS, POTS, STOP

C	A	R	P
A	U	O	O
T	T	I	D
S	O	B	S

Hangman (Get creative and only use naughty words)
Each player takes a turn picking a word to spell out and draws lines underneath to represent the letters in the word. The other person guesses letters. Any letters that fit in the word, get put into the word. The other letters are placed on top above the image and parts of a stick man are drawn till either the word is guessed or stick man is Fucked.

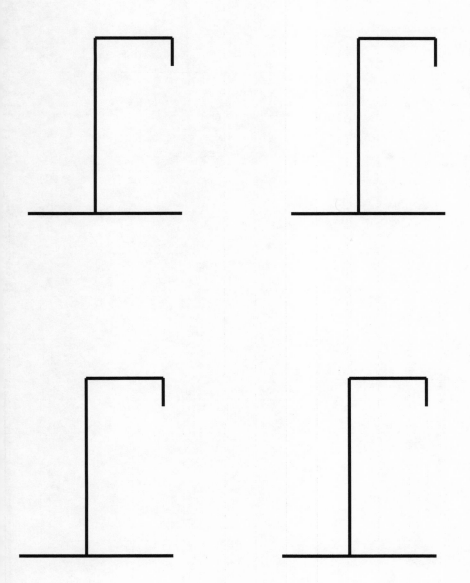

Each player takes a turn writing an 'S' or 'O' in a square. The goal is to complete the sequence S-O-S in three adjacent squares (vertical, horizontal, diagonal). When a player completes the sequence, they mark it as theirs. Play continues until all squares are occupied. Player with the most S-O-S sequences is the winner, bitch tits.

This a jackass puzzle where all the letters have for some goddamn reason fallen to the bottom, lazy assholes. They got then got fucking mixed up on their way down, idiots, but remain in the same row. Complete the puzzle by filling the letters into the column they fall under. You start by filling in the one-letter columns, because that shit doesn't have anywhere else to go in their column. Also try filling in common one-, two- and three-letter words as shown in the wicked tits example below.

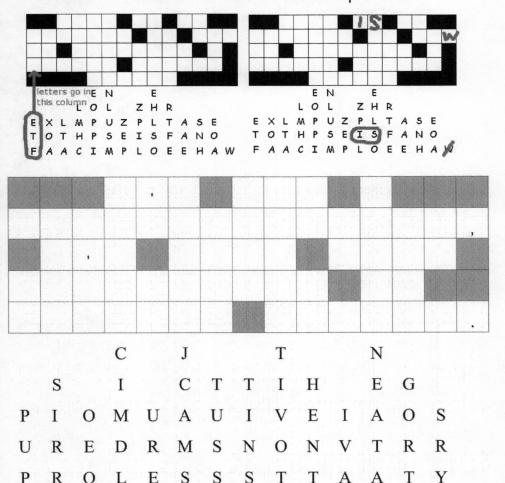

Draw the other half, then maybe color that shit.
This one's going to take a damn while so make sure
you have lots of shit on your plate before you start!

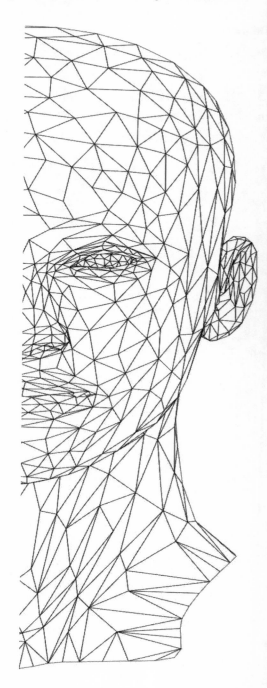

Find the 13 fucking flying fish hidden in image.
Is it just me or are these dickwads creepy as fuck?
Hurry up and find this shit then steer clear.

Answer on page 106

Solve this last motherfucking maze already.
Start at the top and work your way to the bottom

Answer on page 106

Math Squares

Oh my god! Look at this fucked up mess of a puzzle. Good fucking luck trying to fill in the missing numbers.

Use the numbers 1 through 9 to complete the equations.

Each row is a math equation. Work your way from left to right. Can anyone figure this shit out?
Each column is a math equation. Work from top to bottom. I'm out and maybe you should be too!

2	x		-	6	/		**6**
+		x		x		x	
	-	4	x		+	9	**12**
-		+		-		/	
1	+		x	8	+		**46**
x		/		-		x	
	x	8	+		/	1	**63**
42		**5**		**3**		**3**	

Answer on page 107

Color these damn nuts and holes.

This is the last fucking time you have to figure out how to fit the dickweed bricks into the square without changing their shape or breaking them into pieces.

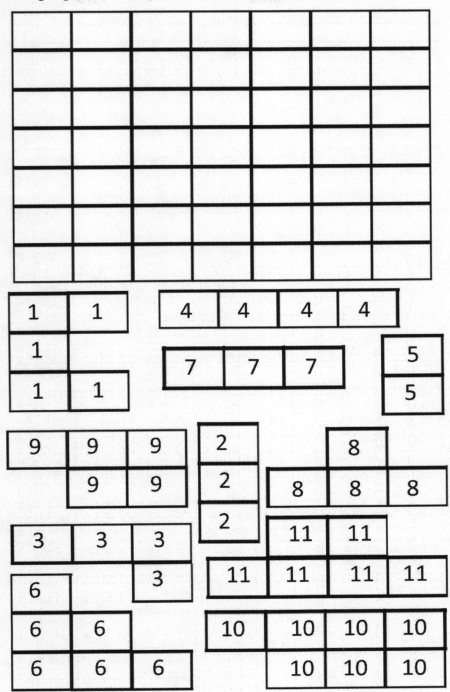

Answer on page 107

I am so tired of explaining this shit to you, but here it is again. You are given a piece of text where each letter is substituted with a number and you need to decide which letters in the alphabet are being coded by the damn numbers you are given. The same fucking example is shown here:

A	B	C	D	E	F	G	H	I	J	K	L	M
		2			16		13	9				10

N	O	P	Q	R	S	T	U	V	W	X	Y	Z
5	1				22	3	7					

T H I S   I S   S O
3 13 9 22   9 22   22 1

M U C H?   F U N .
10 17 2 13   16 17 5

A	B	C	D	E	F	G	H	I

J	K	L	M	N	O	P	Q	R

S	T	U	V	W	X	Y	Z

```
 F  ___ ___ ___     ___      ___ ___ ___ ___ ___ ___
  4   9  12  26      7        3   1   9  25  10  20

___ ___ ___ ___ ___ ___ ___ ___ ___ ___ ___ ___ ___ ___
 3   9  12   2   9   7   6  15  21  24   7  15  21  12  24

    ___ ___ ___ ___ ___ ___ ___ ___ ___
     6  15   7  24  22   3  12  21  24  15

___ ___ ___ ___ ___     ___ ___ ___     ___ ___ ___ ___
15  12  22   7  20       8   7   6      16  25  25  24

___     ___ ___ ___ ___     ___ ___ ___ ___ ___ ___ ___
 7      14  21  10  22       6   1   2   2  25   6   6
```

I'm sure that at about this time in book you could use some damn caffeinated inspiration. Find the french press below that matches it's shadow here on the left.

Answer on page 107

OMG, Fucking find the black boxes in each grid already

The figures given on the side and in top of the grid show the damn numbers of black boxes in that line or column.

For fucks sake it's simple, 3,3 on the left of a line indicates that there is, from left to right, a block of 3 black boxes then a second block of 3 black boxes on the same line. To solve a puzzle, one needs to determine which cells will be boxes and which will be empty. Determining which cells are to be left empty is as important as those to be filled.

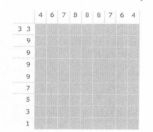 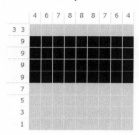 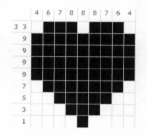

	2	5, 2	1, 2	1, 1, 1, 1	1, 1, 2, 2, 1	1, 2, 1, 1	1, 1	1, 1, 1, 1, 1	1, 1, 2, 2, 1	1, 2, 1, 1	1, 1	1, 1, 1, 1, 1	1, 1, 2, 2, 1	1, 2, 1, 1	1, 1	1, 1	6
4																	
3, 1																	
4, 1																	
1, 3, 1																	
1, 3, 1, 1																	
1, 1, 1, 1																	
1, 3, 1, 3, 1																	
1, 1, 3, 1																	
1, 1, 1																	
1, 3, 1																	
1, 3																	
3, 3																	
2, 3																	
2																	

76

Answer on page 107

Zig Zag is a shit game that I hate fucking making
Complete the 8-letter word at the top of each diagram.
Use the last two letters of the first word as the first two
letters of the second word If you get stuck, try starting at
the bottom of the diagram and working your way up, in
reverse. In other words, do it up the ass instead.

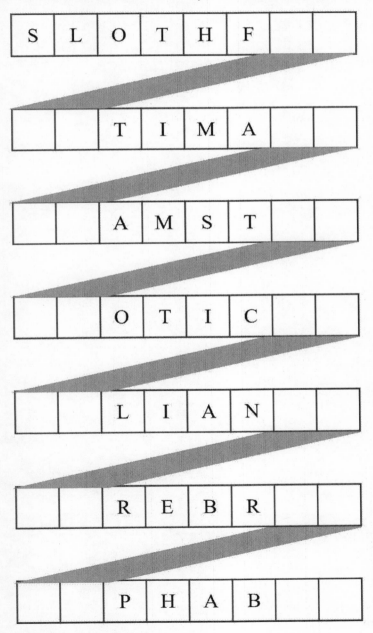

Answer on page 107

Number Blocks

Fuck me sideways, these fuckers keep getting bigger and bigger. How are you going to fill in the missing numbers this time? You're fucking on your own here.

The missing numbers are integers from 1 to 9.
The numbers in each row add up to totals to the right.
The numbers in each column add up to the totals along the bottom. So many fucking numbers.
The diagonal lines also add up the totals to the right.

						29
	6	1		2	6	28
8			6	5	1	27
7	4	9		7		38
3		6	2		4	31
2	3		7	3		27
	8	3	1		9	26
30	33	28	28	30	28	37

Answer on page 107

Unscramble each of the words.
I had some goddman fun and made up some of my
own words in the scrambles just to fuck with you!

1. nards outi   _____

2. noon bite sis 'ut   _____

3. ram chaw air   _____

4. rent dicks dai   _____

5. dilto barey   _____

6. fog nard's eete   _____

7. nurd norau   _____

8. ref ginah   _____

9. lofd foh   _____

10. man dog nd't iave   _____

11. dise tell   _____

12. tang wigamie   _____

13. may tip roelf   _____

14. silly-hlalyhs   _____

Answer on page 107

Letter Tiles – Are you still even fucking here?

Move the tiles around to make the correct phrase.
The three letters on each tile must stay together
and in the given order. Tits to you for getting this far!

O V D	.	O F	N G S	H A U
E R Y	A N	I ' V	N K I	E R -
T I N	A V	N G	I ' M	R O C
E X	T H I	B U	A T I	A D
D P	S Y	T H I	D A Y	R A S
E H	N G .	S T E		

Answer on page 107

80

Find the 1 fucking loser that is different from the rest

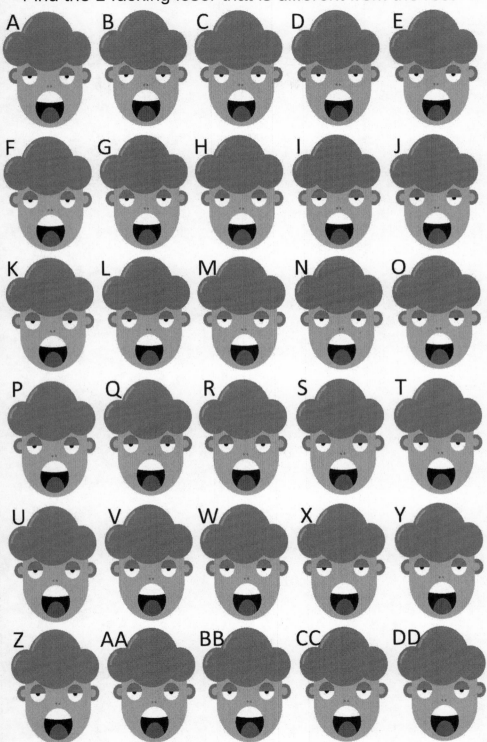

Answer on page 107

Search the damn words in the z already, I'm bored as hell

defer   drag   listless   lag
prolong   stall   laze   lazy
mosey   amble   dally
loser   idle   lounge

```
C X E O P L N G F G W C O A U T E E X B
S O P L D Z Q G A G V X Y M P G D N B V
X B N M I J H L D S R Y I B B C O I Y T
B V E Q W S V H J B V C F L J D R A G F
Y T L S X V T M J H P C P E N B P Q V P
P F D X S R Y L K H F S V C O P L P L M
V P I K L O F T E T U O P R W X P R S E
L M M C E T U O L S G P F H J R E S O L
S E C M L O G F D W S G J M B F R X E I
                        U V W S P E S O
                        W P P Y N E X B
                    L J H L Y M N B
                    W R L L J H I Y
                  S X A P M J G O
                  X D R Y I K B Q
                H K L O F T W E
                T D E F E R L E
              L J M L O G F D
              D W V N J L M E
            V X Y M H J K F
            R Y I J L N B U
          B V C F H C O P
          H P C P E R W X
        K H F S G C H J
        W T U N P R S O
      O L J O P F H X
      F D L X G J M B
    V C O P O O F T
    P R W X P T U O
  P P H J K E O G
  G J M B E Z A L
S Z U V W S P W
O S W P L M N O
P U R E D N L T Y M N B D H S O P B C X
O P L N G F D W C O I U T E X B M E S O
L D Z Q G J N V X Y M P G D B O X E X B
M L A Z Y D S R Y I J B C O S T E N B V
Q W R V H J B V C F H J K E P F H I L T
S X V P M J H P C P L N Y P V P I O L F
E D N L T Y M N B D H S O P B C X B A X
N G F E G N U O L T E X B N E S O Y T E
Q G J N V X Y M P G D B V X E X B P S H
```

Answer on page 108

How many shapes of any goddamn kind can you find in the circle below? And I mean any shape. It's not that hard, you can do this one.
Plus you're almost done and can buy another one of my fucking books so I'm not broke as fuck!

Answer on page 108

Fuck this Fucking Quest

Answer on page 108

Your task is to fill every empty cell with a positive or negative integer in such a way so that each white cell's value equals the sum of its adjoining half-height cells. When complete, each Balance Quest puzzle grid will "balance" itself in such a way so that the four center cells surrounding the center "zero cell" will always add up to zero.

There are five rules that must be followed in every Quest puzzle:
The gray cells must include all integers between -16 and 16, except 0
No number can be repeated within any of the gray cells. SHIT NO!
The number in each white cell must equal the sum of its adjoining cells. The center Zero cell is always the sum of all four adjacent cells.

** Numbers can (and will) be reused across both white and gray cells. The rules specify only that the -16 to 16 numbers can never be used more than once in the gray cells. The same damn example is below:

-8		-8+6=-2		-2+4=-2			2+-9+
	-2	-1+5=4	-2		2	-1	-1+8=0
6				2		0	
5							
	4		4		-9	8	
-1							

1	-13					9	10
-8		-34					11
2					23		-15
						-9	-9
15	31					-3	
-7				0			-10
3	-13	-3					13
14			-2			18	
8					-14		4
	-8					-15	-4

Draw this fucker back in pieces, not sure he wants it

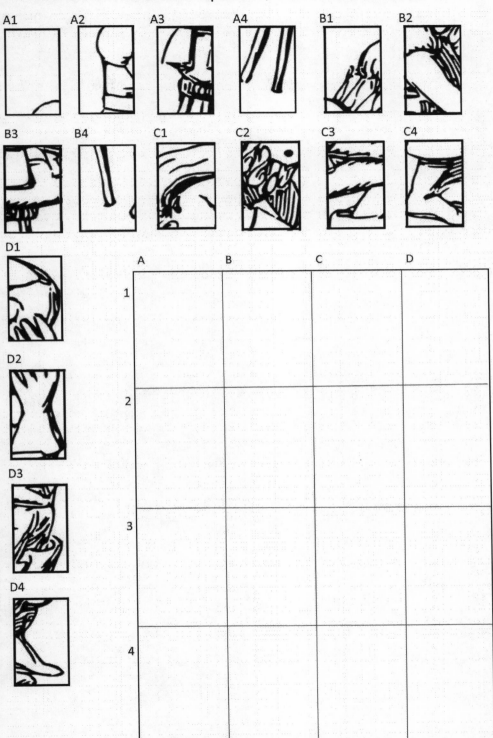

Image on page 108

Connect the dots from 100 to 115, yes only 115. I'm out of ideas to draw! Don't let the extra numbers fool you!

144
218   230   278   240   128   276
100   258   268
270   233   248   249   245   244   243
116   233   242   238
238   246   223   246   264   253   123   237   237
254   245   247   250   237   237
251 257   120   255   255   274   239   272 262   239
254   279   254   185   275   201 236
101   102   226   248   166   200
271
262 265   230   264   117   236   168   167   249   131
256 238   269   250   258   259   257   169   265
241   104   212   243   272   269
259 242   241   122   214   171   247   210   269   266
239   253   222   215   239   170   241   267
244   121   125   107   106   195   172   268   260
239
237 236   119   105   256   250   245   181
236   103   226   271   174   263
268 225   211   277   197   275   236   188   263 236
235
217   261   210   198   109 118 175 176 240
235   266   207   108
124 279   130 215   213   271   278   261 248   178 177
259   196 238   214   189   199   186   187   179
234   265   264   276   273   260 184 183   182 180
260 228
263 266   278   217   110   206   111 273 275   194   213
132   256   231   218   209   267 237   249
277 220
270   261   227   247   270   208   274   246 252   193
262 279   229   112   251 115   252
129   209 238   237   228   225 190   202   127
234   224 252   244   242   191   192   126
227   114   211
272 173 257   274   145   238   255   205   231
216   258   220
267 251   204
140   134 139   253   224   273 113   137
138   135   133   136

Answer on page 108

86

How many words can you find within the words:

I have so much shit to do

1. _____
2. _____
3. _____
4. _____
5. _____
6. _____
7. _____
8. _____
9. _____
10. _____
11. _____
12. _____
13. _____
14. _____
15. _____
16. _____
17. _____
18. _____
19. _____
20. _____
21. _____
22. _____
23. _____
24. _____
25. _____

These my last twatbag rules of sudoku

Numbers from 1 to 9 are inserted into sets that have 9 x 9 = 81 squares in whole. Every shit number can be used just once in every damn 3x3 block, column and row.

- Every number can be used just once in the blocks of 3 x 3 = 9 square blocks. JUST ONCE, dammit!
- Each row of 9 numbers ought to contain all digits 1 through 9 in any order. Don't leave any fucker out.
- Every column of 9 numbers should comprise all digits 1 through 9 in any order. Good fucking luck!

One way to figure out which numbers can go in each space is to use "process of elimination" by checking to see which other numbers are already included within each square – since there can be no duplication of numbers 1-9 within each square (or row or column).

6				3	8	5		
	8		6		7	3		
			5				6	
7		8	4			6		
1								2
		9			1	4		7
	1				5			
		2	7		6		8	
		3	2	1				5

   Answer on page 108

Find the 13 differences between the two lushes

Answer on page 109

These are the shit rules for playing Numbers in a Square

For this problem use only the numbers 1, 2, 3, 4and 5 to solve. The numbers in each heavily outlined set of squares, called cages, must combine (in any order) to produce the damn target number in the top corner using the mathematical operation indicated (+, -, ×, ÷). This is almost too fucking much for me to explain. I need a break. OK, now use each number only once per row, once per column. Cages with just one square should be filled in with the target number in the top corner. A number can be repeated within a cage as long as it is not in the same row or column. I'm so glad that shit is done. Now get to filling this in so you can procrastinate the day away.

8+		4x	12+	
6x				3÷
	6x	9+		
1-		15x		2÷
	2			

   Answer on page 109

Tic Tac Toe to your hearts damn desire.
Take turns placing your mark (o or x) in a square in the grid. The first
person to get three in a row wins. If all 9 squares are filled in before
someone gets three in a row, the game ends in a fucked up tie.

Connect Four – this is the last page of it, so don't waste that shit
Players take turns initialing each cunt circle, starting with the bottom
row, but players can then place the damn discs anywhere as long as
the spaces under them are filled. The winner is the player who gets
four discs in a vertical, horizontal or diagonal row.

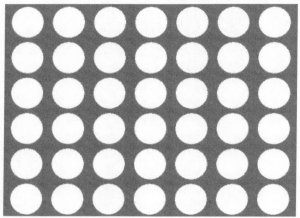

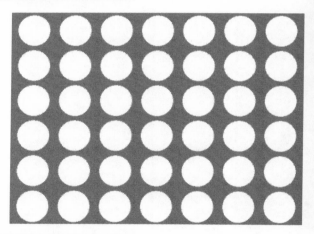

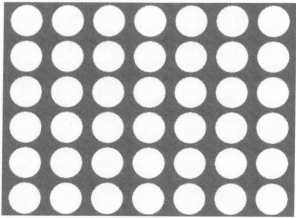

Pipelayer – Go ahead and lay that pipe. You know what I mean
One player is squares the other is circles. Each player takes turns
drawing a horizontal or vertical line between two of their shapes.
The goal is to be the first to create a single continuous line from one
edge of the grid to the other (7-units). You cannot draw one line
across another, so blocking the others move can be an advantage.

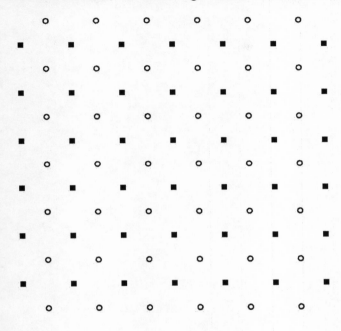

Dots and Boxes – Put your initials in all damn boxes you can
Take turns drawing lines between two adjacent dots with a horizontal
or vertical line. The play who completes the fourth side of the box,
initials the box and gets to draw another line. When all the boxes are
completed the winner is the player who has initialed the most boxes.

Sim that shit up and waste your day away with this damn game
Players alternately join hthe fucking dots on a hexagon by drawing
along the lines provided; the first player who is forced to complete a
triangle in their own color loses. So don't lose, bitch!

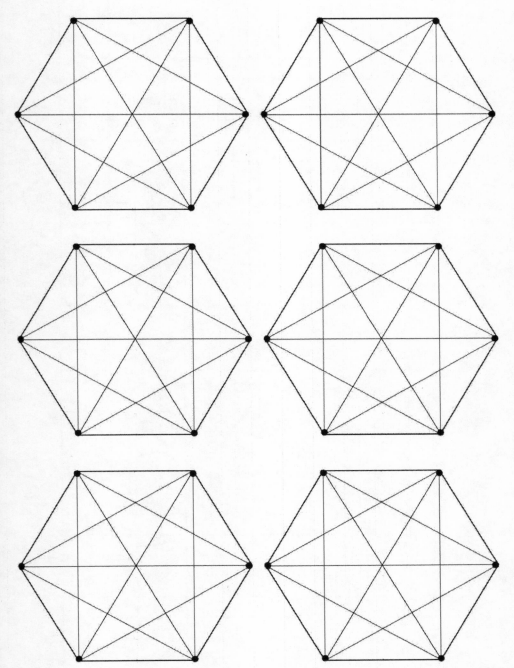

Five in a Row is for all you fuckers who love tic tac toe
The players take turns in marking a square with their x or o.
The first player to get five squares in a row, horizontally,
vertically, or diagonally, wins. (Two games here)

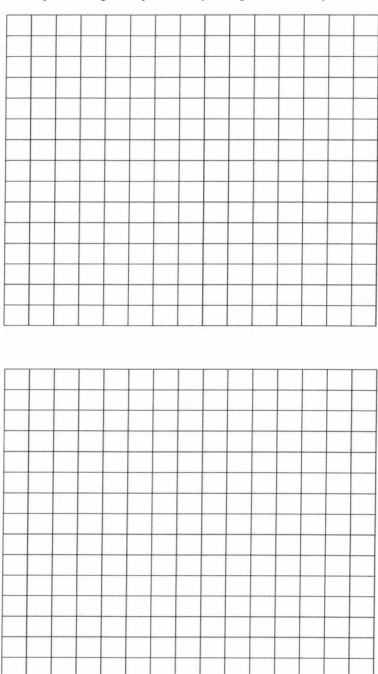

Players take turns in naming a letter. As each letter is named each player must write it immediately into one of the cells in their own grid. Players can choose any letter they like, and letters can be repeated. When the grid is full the players count up the number of four-letter words they have made, reading across, down, or diagonally, and the one with the highest score wins. Tip: you can either choose letters to help you complete words, or you can fuck up your opponent's words.

This player earns 6 points with these words: CARD, TOSS, COAT, RIPS, DOTS, and CUPS

C	A	R	D
O	U	I	O
A	B	P	T
T	O	S	S

This player wins with 7 points from these words: CARP, AUTO, CATS, SOBS, PODS, POTS, STOP

C	A	R	P
A	U	O	O
T	T	I	D
S	O	B	S

Hang the mother fucking man if you don't guess the word
Each player takes a turn picking a word to spell out and draws lines
underneath to represent the letters in the word. The other person
guesses letters. Any letters that fit in the word, get put into the word.
The other letters are placed on top above the image and parts of a
stick man are drawn till the word is guessed or stick man is well hung.

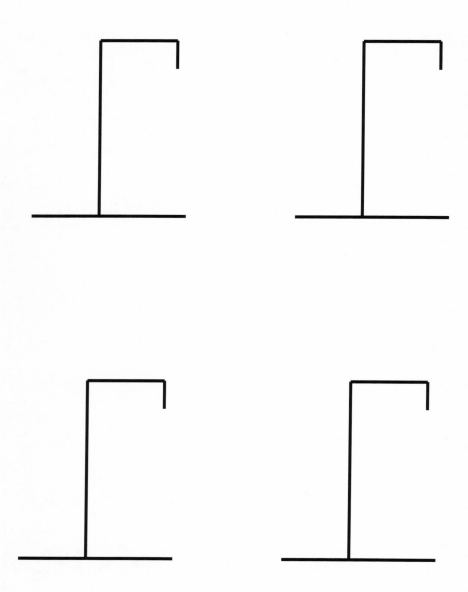

Each player takes a turn writing an 'S' or 'O' in a square. The goal is to complete the damn sequence S-O-S in three adjacent squares (vertical, horizontal, diagonal). When a player completes the shitty sequence, they mark it as theirs. Play continues until all squares are occupied. Player with the most S-O-S sequences is the winner.

Countdown: This is the end bitches! Last Fucking Activity.
The players take turns in choosing letters until there are 9. They
then try to construct a word using just those letters. Each word
scores one point per letter, or double for a nine-letter word. In the
case of a draw both players score. Now go buy another damn book

Page 1

If I applied myself as much as I procrastinated, wow, that would be powerful.

Page 3   **Page 4**

Page 5

9	/	3	+	8	11
-		x		/	
7	-	4	x	2	6
+		/		+	
5	-	6	x	1	-1

7		2		5

Page 7

2	4	4	4	6	6	6
2	2	4	1	1	6	6
7	7	7	1	1	1	6
7	5	5	3	3	3	8
10	10	5	9	11	9	8
10	10	5	9	11	9	8
10	10	5	9	9	9	8

Page 8

I got so much procrastinating done today.

Page 9

F

Page 10

	5	1,1	1,1,1	1,2,1,1	1,2,1,1	1,2,1,1	1,1	1,2,1,1	1,2,1,1	1,1,1	1,1	5
5												
1, 1												
1, 1												
1, 2, 2, 1												
1, 3, 3, 1												
1, 1												
1, 1												
1, 5, 1												
1, 1												
1, 1												
5												

Page 11

S	P	I	R	I	T

I	T	A	L	I	C

I	C	E	M	A	N

A	N	I	M	A	L

A	L	T	I	C	A

C	A	N	D	I	D

I	D	I	O	T	S

Page 12

				22
3	4	5	8	20
2	1	6	7	16
4	7	9	2	22
1	6	8	5	20
10	18	28	22	18

Page 13

1. procrastinate
2. unconcerned
3. unenthusiastic
4. melancholic
5. indifferent
6. lackadaisical
7. dispassionate
8. disinterested
9. unprejudiced
10. disconsolate
11. languishing
12. perfunctory
13. inattentive
14. melancholy

Page 14

I think I still have some unfinished procrastinating to do from yesterday.

Page 15

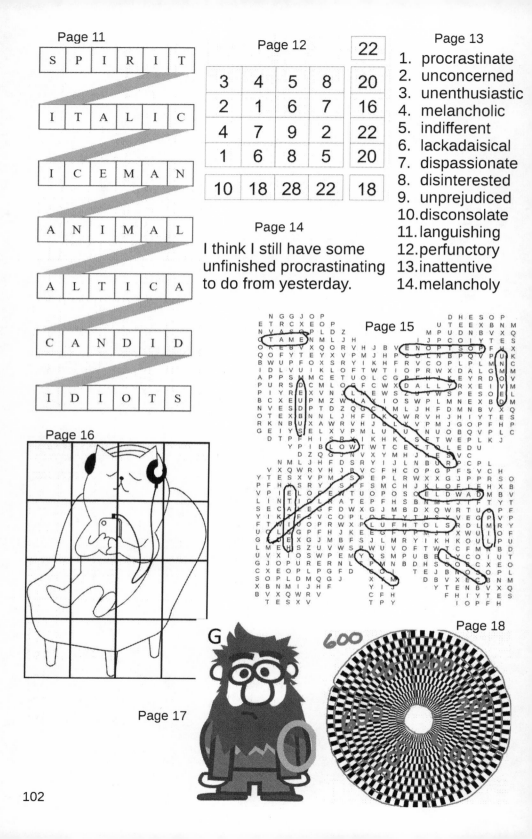

Page 16

Page 17

Page 18

102

Page 19

16	8	-5	-24	0	42	33	21	15
-8								6
1	-13						12	7
-14		-19						5
-7	-8					9	8	14
-1								-6
-2	-11						1	-12
-9								13
8	5	-23	-18		0	-21	-12	4
-3								-16
-13	-28						-9	2
-15								-11
9	-1					21	15	12
-10								3
-4	6	5					6	-5
10								11

Page 20

Page 21

Page 23

8	3	6	9	5	7	1	2	4
2	7	1	3	8	4	9	6	5
5	9	4	1	2	6	8	7	3
3	2	7	4	6	1	5	9	8
9	1	8	5	7	3	6	4	2
6	4	5	2	9	8	7	3	1
7	6	2	8	4	5	3	1	9
1	8	9	7	3	2	4	5	6
4	5	3	6	1	9	2	8	7

Page 24

3+		6x
1	2	3
3÷		
3	1	2
2	**4+**	
2	3	1

Page 34

Procrastination: Hard work pays off after time, but laziness pays off now.

Page 36

Page 37

5	x	9	/	3	15
x		+		+	
4	-	7	x	8	-24
/		-		/	
2	-	6	+	1	-3

10	10	11

Page 38
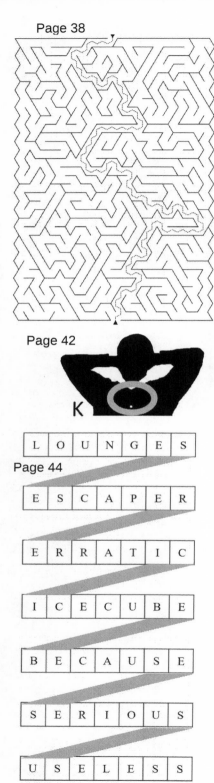

Page 40

2	5	5	5	10	10	10
2	5	5	7	7	10	1
2	5	7	7	7	10	1
2	9	9	7	7	3	1
6	9	9	3	3	3	4
6	6	11	11	11	4	4
6	6	11	11	11	8	8

Page 41
I was going to procrastinate today, but I'll just do it tomorrow.

Page 42
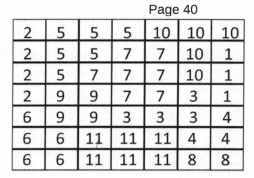

Page 43
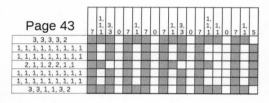

Page 44

LOUNGES

ESCAPER

ERRATIC

ICECUBE

BECAUSE

SERIOUS

USELESS

Page 45

7	3	5	8	4	27
5	1	9	2	6	23
4	3	6	8	7	28
7	8	2	1	9	27
3	6	5	4	8	26
26	21	27	23	34	23

(23)

Page 46

I'm not a procrastinator, I just prefer doing all my work in a deadline-induced panic.

Page 47

104

Page 48

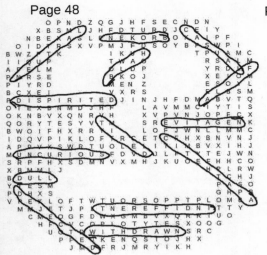

Page 49

1. watch the clock
2. dilly-dally
3. bum around
4. diddle-daddle
5. fool around
6. fritter away
7. get nowhere fast
8. turned off
9. goof off
10. hang around
11. hang out
12. put off
13. scrounge around
14. shlep along

Page 50

1	13	4	24	4	18	5
12						13
-5	-9				-6	-10
-4						4
11	13	20		-8	-20	-11
2						-9
-3	7		0		12	14
10						-2
-12	-3	-24		-13	-22	-14
9						-8
-6	-21				9	6
-15		-52	24			3
-13	-5			37	31	15
8		-28				16
-7	-23				6	-1
-16						7

Page 51   59 Total

Page 52

Page 53

Page 55

1	7	3	2	4	6	9	5	8
8	5	2	1	7	9	3	4	6
4	6	9	8	5	3	1	7	2
9	1	7	6	3	8	5	2	4
6	2	4	5	9	1	8	3	7
3	8	5	7	2	4	6	9	1
5	9	6	4	8	7	2	1	3
2	4	1	3	6	5	7	8	9
7	3	8	9	1	2	4	6	5

Page 56

Page 57

2-	2-		8x
	3	1-	
8x	3+		
		4+	

Page 67

I'm not a procrastinator, I'm just very productive at useless things.

Page 69

Page 70

106

Page 71

2	x	9	-	6	/	2	6
+		x		x		x	
5	-	4	x	3	+	9	12
-		+		-		/	
1	+	4	x	8	+	6	46
x		/		-		x	
7	x	8	+	7	/	1	63
42		5		3		3	

Page 73

6	9	9	9	3	3	3
6	6	9	9	11	11	3
6	6	6	11	11	11	11
1	1	7	7	7	5	2
1	10	10	10	10	5	2
1	1	10	10	10	8	2
4	4	4	4	8	8	8

Page 74

From a purely procrastination standpoint. Today has been a wild success.

Page 75

Page 76

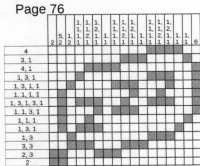

Page 77

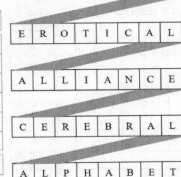

S L O T H F U L

U L T I M A T E

T E A M S T E R

E R O T I C A L

A L L I A N C E

C E R E B R A L

A L P H A B E T

Page 78

						29
9	6	1	4	2	6	28
8	5	2	6	5	1	27
7	4	9	8	7	3	38
3	7	6	2	9	4	31
2	3	7	7	3	5	27
1	8	3	1	4	9	26
30	33	28	28	30	28	37

Page 79

1. sit around
2. sit on one's butt
3. warm a chair
4. sick and tired
5. be dilatory
6. drag one's feet
7. run around
8. hang fire
9. hold off
10. don't give a damn
11. let slide
12. waiting game
13. play for time
14. shilly-shally

Page 80

I'm exhausted. I've had a very busy day of over-thinking things and procrastinating.

Page 81

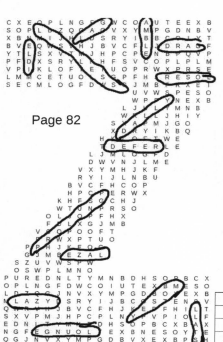

Page 82

Page 83

219

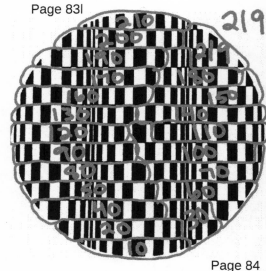

Page 84

-14	-13	-34	-13	0	23	32	9	-1
1								10
-8	-21						23	11
-13								12
2	-10	21				-9	-6	-15
-12								9
16	31						-3	-9
15								6
-7	-13	-3	-2		-8	6	-12	-2
-6								-10
3	10						18	13
7								5
14	9	1				-14	1	-3
-5								4
8	-8						-15	-11
-16								-4

Page 85

Page 86

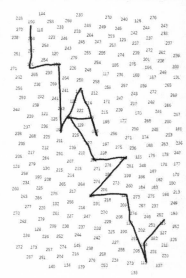

Page 88

6	2	4	1	3	8	5	7	9
9	8	5	6	2	7	3	1	4
3	7	1	5	9	4	2	6	8
7	3	8	4	5	2	6	9	1
1	4	6	9	7	3	8	5	2
2	5	9	8	6	1	4	3	7
4	1	7	3	8	5	9	2	6
5	9	2	7	4	6	1	8	3
8	6	3	2	1	9	7	4	5

Page 89

Page 90

8+ 1	3	4x 4	12+ 2	5
6x 2	4	1	5	3÷ 3
3	6+ 5	9+ 2	4	1
1- 4	1	15x 5	3	2÷ 2
5	2 2	3	1	4

Great Fucking Job
You finished the
Whole damn thing!

Thank you for your fucking damn purchase!!
I hope you found this shit fun as hell.

If you leave a review on Amazon and email me to let
me know, I will send you a free paperback copy of any
book of your choice from my Amazon collection!

http://www.amazon.com/T.L.-Adams/e/B00YSROGC4

tamaraadamsauthor@gmail.com

www.tamaraladamsauthor.com

Check out these other items by the Tamara:

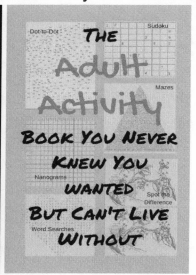

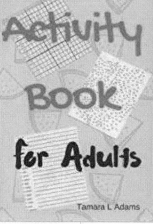

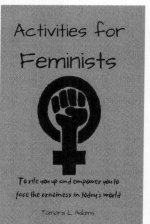

Books by Tamara L Adams

Angry Journal
Art Up This Journal
Backstabbing Bitches: Adult Activities
Puptivities: Adult Activities
Cativities: Adult Activities
Activititties: Adult Activities
I Hate My Boss: Adult Activities
Activity Book for Adults
Activity Book You Never Knew You Wanted But Can't Live Without
Activity Book You need to Buy Before You Die
Fuck I'm Bored : Adult Activity Book
I'm Still Fucking Bored
The Activity Book That Will Transform Your Life
Activities to do while you number two
Timmy and the Dragon
Unmotivated Coloring
Angry Coloring
Coloring Happy Quotes
Inspirational Quotes Coloring
Coloring Cocktails
Cussing Creatures Color
101 Quote Inspired Journal Prompts
Unlocking Happiness Planner
Daily Fitness Planner
Bloggers Daily Planner
Bloggers Daily Planner w margins
Writers Daily Planner
Writers Daily Planner w coloring
Busy Mothers Planner
Where's Woody Coloring Book
99 Writing Prompts
Deciding Destiny: Christy's Choice
Deciding Destiny: Matt's Choice
Deciding Destiny: Lindsays Choice
Deciding Destiny: Joe's Choice
Rich Stryker: Julie's Last Hope
Rich Stryker: Tom's Final Justice
Unlocking Happiness
Getting to Know Yourself Journal
#2 Getting to Know Yourself Journal